ANNI'S INDIA DIARY

Things to Pack

paintbox, pencils
compass
sunglasses
T-shirts
shorts
sandals
swimsuit
sun cream
camera
sneakers
toothbrush ← Mom wrote that
and my diary!

Pakistan

For Mom & Dad,
with love from Anni

A TRELD BICKNELL BOOK

Published by Whispering Coyote Press Inc.
P.O. Box 2159, Halesite, New York 11743-2159

Printed in Singapore by Imago Publishing

Library of Congress Cataloging-in-Publication Data

Axworthy, Anni.

Anni's India diary/by Anni Axworthy.

p. cm.

Summary: A ten-year-old's diary entries chronicle the magical sights
and sounds she and her family encounter as they explore India.
ISBN 1-879085-59-3: $14.95
(1. India—fiction. 2. Diaries—fiction.) I. Title.
PZ7. A9616An 1992
(Fic)—dc20   92-17624   CIP   AC

Text set in Souvenir Light
by Chambers Wallace

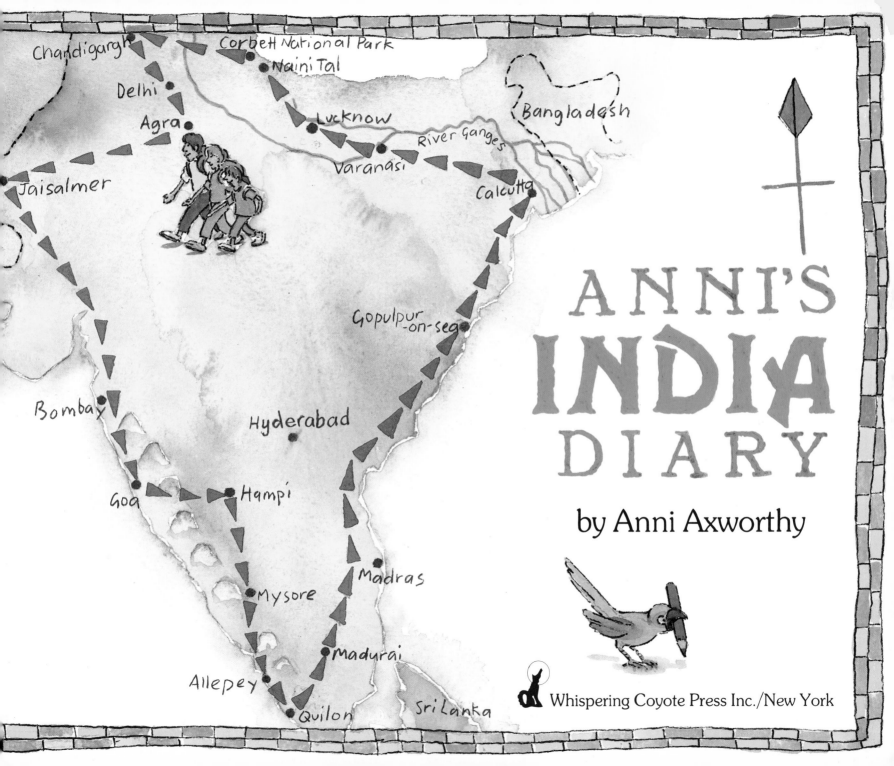

Chandigargh

Corbett National Park

Naini Tal

Delhi

Lucknow

Agra

Bangladesh

River Ganges

Varanasi

Jaisalmer

Calcutta

Gopulpur-on-sea

ANNI'S
INDIA
DIARY

by Anni Axworthy

Bombay

Hyderabad

Goa

Hampi

Mysore

Madras

Madurai

Allepey

Whispering Coyote Press Inc./New York

Quilon

Sri Lanka

October 10

Delhi My name is Anni. Today is my first day in India. When I woke up, I felt very mixed up. I couldn't remember where I was. Then I heard bicycle bells, car horns, and people shouting words I didn't understand. Dad was yelling into the telephone and Mom was trying to get some hot water out of the faucet in the bathroom. I am going to put everything down in my new diary.

We go out to see the city. In the street Mom and Dad hold my hands tightly. I guess they feel strange, too. We ride through Delhi in an auto rickshaw. I squeeze right in the middle. I love swerving through the crowded streets. Mom shuts her eyes every time she sees a cow wandering in the traffic. Our driver honks his horn as we sway from side to side—it's great! I wish I could drive a rickshaw sometime.

GANDHI CENTENARY
1869-1969
75 P. भारत INDIA

Ph. 33
NNY GUEST HOUSE
USE, C. PLACE, NEW DELHI.
Dated

October 11

Mom, Dad, and I go to the bazaar to buy things for our train journey. The street is crowded with people—riding, walking, selling, or just sitting on the pavement. We squeeze past bicycle rickshaws, bullock carts, and even an elephant. When Mom chooses some oranges from a stall, a monkey jumps down from the rooftop, grabs the fruit, and runs away. We see a man frying swirls of orange batter in a huge pan. It's called *jalabi*. We buy some. It is soaked in syrup and tastes sweet and delicious.

Alleyways lead off in all directions. Mom and I go to the *sari* shop, while Dad enjoys a cup of tea.

A sari is very long—at least six yards of material. Indian ladies wrap it around themselves to make a beautiful long dress. The salesman helps Mom and me to choose some fabric and then shows us how to wrap our saris. It's quite tricky! We each choose a short blouse called a *choli* to wear underneath. Dad walks straight past the shop and doesn't recognize me!

White cows with large horns wander through the bazaar. I'm not frightened because they look so peaceful, gently nuzzling the ground for vegetable scraps. One cow takes a carrot from a stall, but the trader just waves a stick and smiles. In India cows are holy and no one harms them.

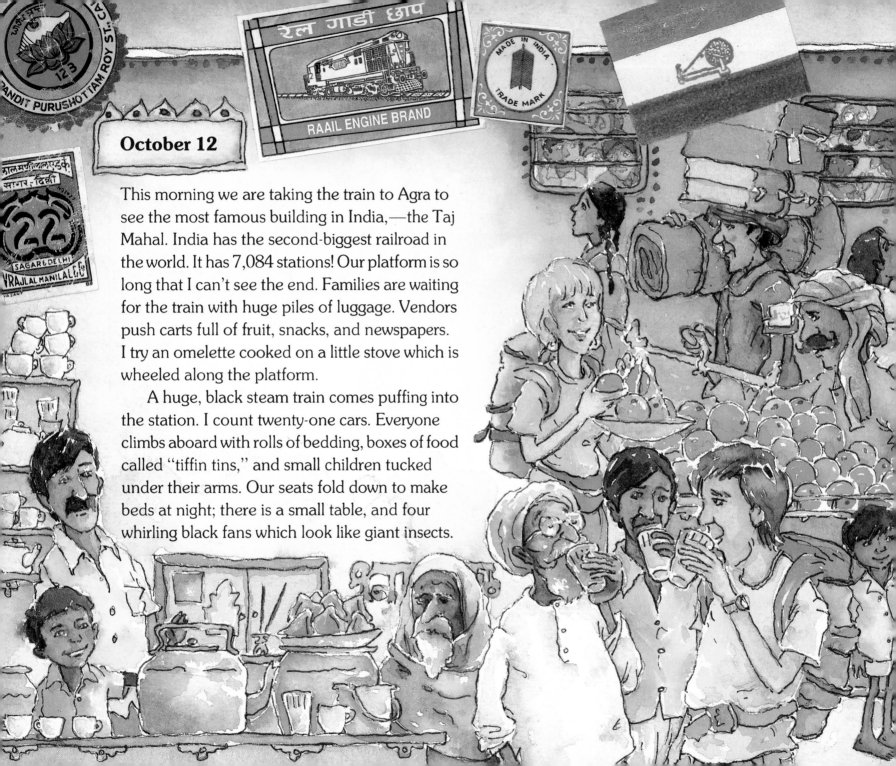

October 12

This morning we are taking the train to Agra to see the most famous building in India,—the Taj Mahal. India has the second-biggest railroad in the world. It has 7,084 stations! Our platform is so long that I can't see the end. Families are waiting for the train with huge piles of luggage. Vendors push carts full of fruit, snacks, and newspapers. I try an omelette cooked on a little stove which is wheeled along the platform.

A huge, black steam train comes puffing into the station. I count twenty-one cars. Everyone climbs aboard with rolls of bedding, boxes of food called "tiffin tins," and small children tucked under their arms. Our seats fold down to make beds at night; there is a small table, and four whirling black fans which look like giant insects.

RAAIL ENGINE BRAND

MADE IN INDIA TRADE MARK

October 12

Neem tree bark is good for brushing your teeth!

Agra We squeeze into a rickshaw and ask the driver to take us to the Taj Mahal. When Mom sees its gleaming white towers, she takes Dad's hand and says it is the most romantic building in the world. He laughs and gives her hand a squeeze. The Taj Mahal is built of white marble, covered with precious stones making patterns of flowers. Long ago there was an emperor called Shah Jahan who loved his wife, Mumtaz Mahal, so much that, when she died, he built this beautiful building in her memory. They are buried together in the basement vault. Their tomb was once lined with gold, but thieves have stolen its gold lining and its silver doors.

Indian squirrel

October 13

The train to Jaisalmer takes a day and a night. We travel through the Thar Desert of Rajasthan. We all sit cross-legged and eat *thali* with our fingers. It is a tray of small bowls filled with rice, curried vegetables, yoghurt, and flat rounds of bread called *chapattis*. It is delicious! My hands get very sticky. The coach attendant brings our bed rolls and helps to make up our berths for the night. The train rocks me to sleep, as I watch the stars and the cooking fires in distant villages.

No. 091120

दक्षिण रेलवे
SOUTHERN RAILWAY
बिस्तर कूपन/BED ROLL COU
रु. 5 प्रति रात्रि/Rs. 5 Per Nigh

गाडी सं....... तारीख.....
Train No.   Date

स्टेशन/Station........

वर्थ सं.....
Berth No.   बाला. 2 टियर/प्रथम श्रेणी
             AC-2-T/I Cl. Bogie N

पीएनआर/टिकट सं./PNR/Ticket No.

From.....   से/To.....

यात्री पत्रा
PASSENGER'S FO

October 15

Jaisalmer is an ancient city built of golden sandstone. It was an important stopping place on a trading route between India and eastern Asia when merchants crossed the continent on camels. We are taking a camel journey, too. The drivers load the camels with quilts, firewood, sacks of fodder, and pots and pans. One driver helps me climb into the saddle. Goro, my camel, rocks forward and then backward to straighten his legs. Then he lurches into a standing position. He has pegs through his nose for the reins which I hold very tightly. We set off in a long line, one camel following another.

When we stop for lunch, I help unload the camels and lead Goro to a shady trough for a drink. He gulps, dribbles, and belches loudly. Camels are disgusting!

Two boys with sticks pass by, following a herd of goats. They let me hold a baby goat; it suckles my finger tips. As they head for the rocky hills, the goat bells tinkle a friendly chorus.

Later we stop at a small village of mud huts, with thatched roofs and painted walls. I meet Bodhini. She wears gold earrings, white bangles, and no shoes. Inside her family's hut she shows me the *charpoy*, a cot strung with string, which she shares with her brother and baby sister. The floor is hard packed earth. In the corner stand an oil lamp and a tall water bottle. They have no electricity, and one of Bodhini's chores is to collect water from the village pump every day.

October 25

Goa We take the ferry across the river and ride motorbike-taxis through avenues of palm trees. Pigs and goats dart about in the red soil. The houses are painted ice-cream colors, and all the churches look like giant wedding cakes. We go for a refreshing swim. Dad holds my hand as the warm waves of the Arabian Sea burst over my head, washing away the dirt and dust. A girl called Sheema brings a basket of fruit which she places at our feet. We choose fresh green coconuts which she breaks open with a sharp knife.

32 GOA CRACKERS

jalon

papaya

mango

We have dinner under the stars. Dad really enjoys Indian beer. I've ordered some tiger prawns – I wonder if they look like this?

November 1

Hampi Today we take a train across the western *ghats.* It is so steep that a steam engine has to push us up the hills. Tropical birds dive past waterfalls and monkeys prance through the flowering trees. At Hospet, we squeeze onto a crowded bus, between vegetables, sacks of grain, and even a chicken with its legs bound together.

At Hampi we see the ruins of a huge city, destroyed in 1565. Holy men called *sadhus,* dressed in orange robes, sit in the caves meditating and collecting alms. We leave on the evening bus; there is such a crowd that people climb in through the windows. I follow some boys up a ladder onto the roof of the bus. Mom and Dad are close behind, but they look worried when we have to duck beneath the palm trees. My new friends teach me Hindi songs as we trundle along the dusty road.

November 6

Today we are in **Mysore**, a city scented with flowers and sandalwood. At the bazaar, Mom and I are given garlands to wear in our hair. Dad has a necklace of golden chrysanthemums. I've filled my water bottle because it's very hot and we are going to climb the one thousand pilgrim steps of Chaumundi Hill. Monkeys and butterflies keep us company.

Halfway up we rest at a statue of Nandi, the black bull ridden by the Hindu god, Shiva. A priest blesses me and puts a blob of red powder on my forehead; this is called *puja*. At the top, we join pilgrims with shaved heads who wait in line with coconuts, bananas, flowers, and coins to present at Shiva's temple.

We visit the sandalwood factory to watch incense sticks being made. Sonu is twelve; he shows me how to roll a thin sliver of bamboo in a paste and then dip it into perfumed powder. Then it is laid outdoors to dry.

Mom buys packets of incense and soap, which make our hotel room smell wonderful.

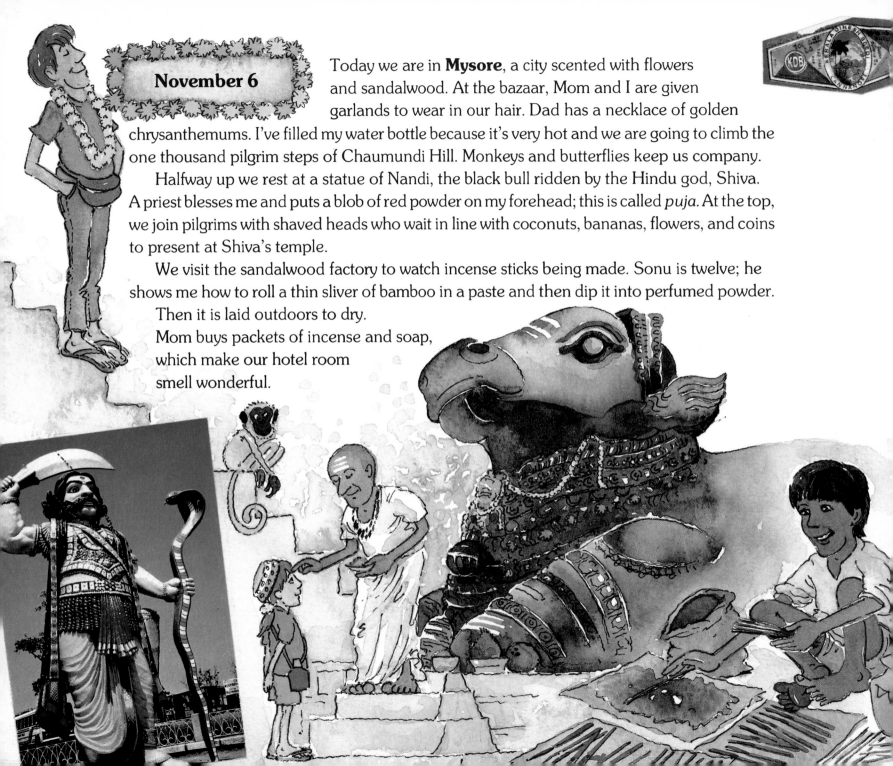

November 10

This is **Kerala**, the land of spices. We take a boat from Allepey through the lagoons and waterways to Quilon. I climb onto the roof with my paint box and wave to the children playing in the shallow waters by the shore. We drift past narrow strips of land with palm trees, thatched huts, cows, chickens, and pigs standing in small gardens. Fishermen wade past with only their heads above water, trawling nets by hand. Long wooden boats float by laden with coconut fiber used for matting and ropes. The sun is setting as we pass giant fishing nets perched on the banks.

November 15

We've come to **Madurai** to see the Meenakshi Temple. There are twelve brightly painted towers surrounded by a wall. We leave our shoes and explore the long halls and corridors. As my eyes grow used to the darkness, I can see stone carvings in all directions. Statues are draped in flowers and melted fat. The rancid smell mixes with the burning incense. Our guide is called Ravi. He tells us that the Meenakshi Temple is named after a princess who lived two thousand years ago. There is a picture of her wedding painted on the ceiling. A priest is blessing a bride and groom; her hands are decorated with patterns made from *henna*, a dye made from vegetables.

Ravi tells us that most Indian marriages are arranged, and parents choose partners for their children. An astrologer reads their horoscopes to see if they will be happy together and chooses the wedding day. I wonder who Mom and Dad would choose for me!

Many temples keep an elephant; the Meenakshi has two. I put a coin on one elephant's trunk, and he rests it on my head. It feels heavy and itchy, but this is his way of blessing me. Inside the temple there are stalls selling bangles, flowers, and toys. Dad says the only thing missing is a café. I try not to giggle.

November 27

We are in Orissa on the eastern coast of India, taking a jeep to **Gopulpur-on-Sea**. It's so crowded Mom and I have to sit on Dad's lap. He suggests that I ride on the roof with our luggage. On the beach the fishermen are bringing in their catch in boats made from split trees roped together. People gather around the piles of silver fish. A girl called Mamani is gathering fish into a basket. She writes her name in the sand and then I write mine. She points at her nose and then at mine and wants to know if I'd like my nose pierced in three places like hers. Mom shakes her head before I can even ask.

school bus

25 यामिनी राय JAMINI ROY
1978
भारत
INDIA

Mamani places a coil of fabric on my head and balances her basket of fish on the top. I have to steady it with my hands as we walk to her village, tucked among the palm groves behind the beach. We go to the market where her mother is waiting to sell the fish. We arrange it on rush mats. Now Mamani must return to the beach to help her father and brothers.

On the way, she shows me the village school, where children are having lessons outside under a shady tree. Mamani and the other children who help their families during the day have their lessons in the evening. They learn math, English, and the geography and history of India. City children wear uniforms and go to school in rickshaw buses.

I think I prefer Mamani's comfortable outdoor school!

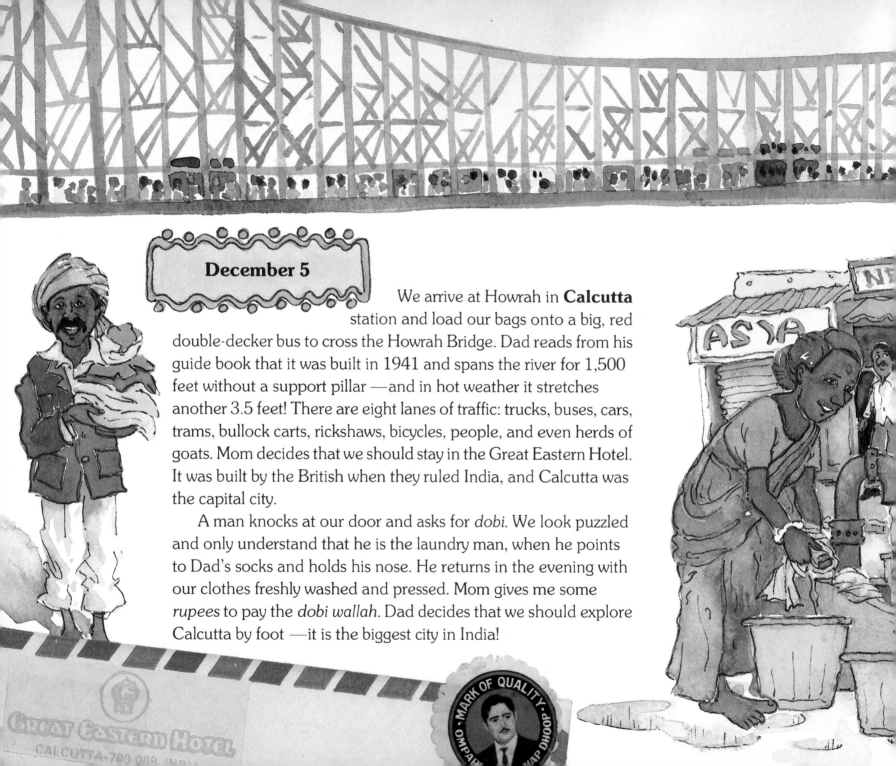

December 5

We arrive at Howrah in **Calcutta** station and load our bags onto a big, red double-decker bus to cross the Howrah Bridge. Dad reads from his guide book that it was built in 1941 and spans the river for 1,500 feet without a support pillar —and in hot weather it stretches another 3.5 feet! There are eight lanes of traffic: trucks, buses, cars, trams, bullock carts, rickshaws, bicycles, people, and even herds of goats. Mom decides that we should stay in the Great Eastern Hotel. It was built by the British when they ruled India, and Calcutta was the capital city.

A man knocks at our door and asks for *dobi*. We look puzzled and only understand that he is the laundry man, when he points to Dad's socks and holds his nose. He returns in the evening with our clothes freshly washed and pressed. Mom gives me some *rupees* to pay the *dobi wallah*. Dad decides that we should explore Calcutta by foot —it is the biggest city in India!

GREAT EASTERN HOTEL
CALCUTTA-700 089 INDIA

MARK OF QUALITY

Outside the hotel we meet a match-seller called Ramu. He is a farmer who brought his family to Calcutta when his crops failed. Many people leave their villages to try and find work in the cities. Ramu washes himself and his small son at the water pump on the street corner. An old lady arrives with a basket of laundry to take her turn at the pump. I say good-night to Ramu. He sings as he builds a roof of plastic sacks to protect his sleeping family.

December 15

We are in the holy city of **Varanasi**. I draw and sometimes help to row our boat along the River Ganges. Mom and Dad are taking pictures of the happy pilgrims, washing away their sins in the sacred river. The steps are also used for washing clothes.

Our boatman tells us that most Indians are Hindu and they have many gods and goddesses. He gives me a little bowl made of leaves which holds a tiny candle resting on marigold leaves. It is very pretty as it floats away on the river; a little gift to the gods.

I'm learning to play cricket. It's a bit like baseball, except that we are using a flat piece of wood for a bat and there are only two bases, called "stumps." I hit the ball into the Ganges and score six runs!

In the narrow alleyways there are shops which sell beautiful kites and big colorful masks of all the gods and goddesses. We each choose one—mine is Ganesh, the Elephant God.

cricket team

Ganesh

Kali

Hanuman

December 23

Naini Tal   We reach Bareilly in the middle of the night. I'm very sleepy and Mom tucks me up in her shawl in the waiting room. It is still dark when we climb aboard the Kumaon Express. As day breaks, blue hills rise from the rocky landscape near Kathgodam.

In a taxi we zigzag through the hills for about twenty miles. Our driver says that these hills are the home of tigers, leopards, and hundreds of kinds of birds. Finally we reach Naini Tal, a hill station where people come to stay in the summer when the city gets too hot.

We ride ponies to the top of Cheena Hill. My pony is called Somi. He picks his way very carefully along the steep, snowy path. Our guide runs along holding the tail of Mom's pony.

Varanasi

Lucknow

Bareilly

Kathgodam

SALEENA sweets

SALEENA

ES 12   PRICE
P. A. ASANARKUNJU   Rs.1·00
QUILON-10

TURK

CLASS 7
DIVISION 2
SUB-DIVISION 1

KAMAL FIREWORKS INDUSTRIES, SIVAKAS

The ride down the path is scarier—Somi is in a hurry for his dinner, and I have to lean back in the saddle to balance when his hoofs slide among the ice and rocks.

December 25

It's Christmas day! I give Dad a fork so that he won't get covered in rice when he eats his thali. Mom's present is a stencil and some henna, so she can decorate her hands like a bride. My gift is a surprise. We row across the lake to the bazaar, where I have my ears pierced. We buy Rajasthani earrings, and now I look just like an Indian girl!

New Year's Day

Ramnagar We collect permits to enter the Corbett National Park, which is famous for protecting tigers. The bus takes us past high fences and deep into the forest.

We set off to explore the park—on the back of a magnificent elephant called Chini, which means sugar. Her driver, or *mahout*, sits on her neck with his feet tucked under her pink, freckled ears. We climb into a *howdah* on Chini's back. It is just like an upturned table with padding. I grab one of the legs and hold on tight as she plods through the long grass. Nearby we hear wood cracking, and no one speaks as we watch a family of wild elephants breakfasting on a clump of trees. My parting gift to Chini is an apple.

Forest Department........................Circle, Uttar Pradesh

LION BRAN
QUALITY FABRICS

January 23

On our way back to Delhi, we stop in **Chandigargh**. We visit the famous Rock Garden, the weirdest garden I have ever been in. It is surrounded by a high wall, and stone birds guard the low arched entrances.

I am soon lost in a magic land of winding paths, bridges, and a pavilion on top of a waterfall. There are spotty dogs made from smashed pottery, concrete monkeys, glittering peacocks, walls of water urns, and wiggly cactus tumbling from pots.

Nek Chand, the man who built it, had a childhood dream: *"Once upon a time a King and Queen lived and loved here, dined and danced, fought and triumphed, and then their kingdom collapsed at the zenith of their power."* He has preserved their kingdom forever in his garden. When I get home, I will save everything that gets broken and make a wonderful garden like this.

January 25

Delhi We choose a grand restaurant for our farewell dinner. Mom and I are wearing our saris. Dad says we look almost as beautiful as the waiters in their big golden turbans. They fill our table with plates of curry, spicy yoghurt, buttery *nan* bread, and hot pickles. I drink a *lassi* made with milk curd and ice, while Mom and Dad smile over their *masala* tea.

I look through the pages of my diary. It's full of all the brilliant places we have visited on our journey. There is only one page left for tomorrow—our last day in India.

January 26

Delhi It's our last day. I try to cram all of my new belongings into my bulging backpack. Outside there are excited crowds of people celebrating Republic Day—India's Independence day. It's very hard to find a taxi to take us to the airport, so we catch a lift on a horse-drawn *tonga* and set off. It's slow going, and we get stuck behind a troop of camels going home from the parade.

Helicopters whirl overhead, dropping rose petals on the dancing crowd, and the sky is filled with red, white, and green balloons trailing Indian flags.

As our plane takes off, I can see Delhi from my window. Fireworks are bursting over the city. I wave good-bye to India and all the friends I have made.

गणतंत्र दिवस परेड
REPUBLIC DAY PARADE

1120

परेड और सांस्कृतिक इ
PARADE AND CULTU

26 जनवरी JANUARY
राजपथ RAJPAT

Chandra
SPARKLERS
10 x 10
100
STICKS
MAHALAXMI